Rosa Parks

Rose attended Alabama State College in Montgomery for a short time.

Mother of the Civil Rights Movement

Rosa Louise McCauley was born in Tuskegee, Alabama on February 4, 1913. While she was still young, she moved with her mother and brother to her grandparents' farm in Pine Level, Alabama.

Unscramble the words in the sentence below to learn more about Rosa's family.

Rosa's _____ was a _____ and
        OETHMR   ECHATER

her _____ was a carpenter.
     ERFAHT

Rose attended Montgomery Industrial School for Girls and graduated from the all-black Booker T. Washington High School in 1928.

Y0-DKP-530

Rosa married Raymond Parks in 1932. Raymond was a barber. Both he and Rosa became active in different civil rights causes, especially black voter rights. Rosa worked with the Youth Council of the National Association for the Advancement of Colored People (NAACP) as a volunteer.

VOTE

Connect the dots to find one of the tools Raymond Parks used as a barber.

1.
2.
21.
3.
20.
4.
5.
6.
7.
8.
19.
9.
18.
13.
12.
11.
10.
17.
16.
14.
15.

Rosa's help in the NAACP led her to be elected as their Montgomery secretary in 1943.

Through her volunteer work with the NAACP, Rosa helped in the efforts to overcome racial segregation in education and also in public places. This was a difficult task and progress was slow.

Since Rosa's work for the NAACP was on a volunteer basis, she had to keep other jobs to pay her bills.

Color the money.

To learn what some of Rosa's paying jobs were, solve the code below.

A	B	C	D	E	F	G	H	I	J	K	L	M
✹	❀	✣	♣	➸	❤	❢	✲	✄	✆	☛	✈	✉

N	O	P	Q	R	S	T	U	V	W	X	Y	Z
✿	✫	✦	✡	✎	❦	☎	✒	✙	✖	✍	✠	✓

___ ___ ___ ___ ___ ___ ___ ___ ___ ___ ___

✲ ✫ ✒ ❦ ➸ ☛ ➸ ➸ ✦ ➸ ✎

and

___ ___ ___ ___ ___ ___ ___ ___ ___ ___

❦ ➸ ✹ ✉ ❦ ☎ ✎ ➸ ❦ ❦

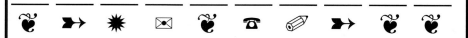

Rosa even sold life insurance for awhile!

Like many others, Rosa depended on the city bus to get to work. In Montgomery, the first ten seats of every bus were for white passengers. Black passengers could not sit in these seats even if there were no whites on the bus.

Color the city bus.

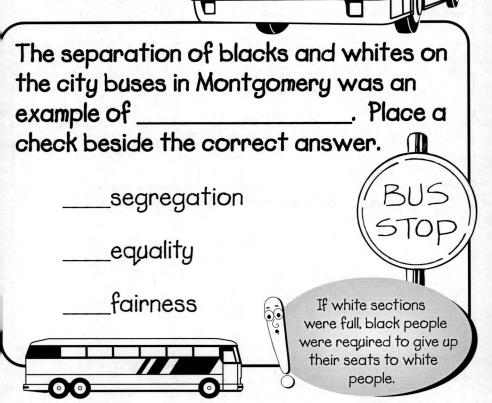

The separation of blacks and whites on the city buses in Montgomery was an example of _____. Place a check beside the correct answer.

____segregation

____equality

____fairness

BUS STOP

If white sections were full, black people were required to give up their seats to white people.

On December 1, 1955, Rosa boarded a bus after a long day at work. She sat in the black section at the rear of the bus, along with three other blacks. When all of the white seats were filled, Rosa and the other black passengers were told to give up their seats as more white passengers got on the bus. Rosa refused.

At first, the other black passengers refused to give up their seats also. When the driver threatened that he would call the police, the three gave up their seats. Rosa still refused and was arrested. She was taken to jail and fined $14.

In what Alabama city did this event take place? Circle your answer.

Tallahassee

Richmond

Montgomery

Rosa's arrest interested E.D. Nixon, a black
community leader. He asked her if
he could use her case to try to
bring an end to segregation
on the buses in Montgomery.
Rosa bravely said, "Yes!"

Rosa's mother
and husband feared
for Rosa's safety if
she agreed to
Nixon's idea.

Find the words in the Word Find below.

ROSA   RIGHTS   BUS

R	L	A	W	R
T	O	B	I	A
T	S	S	N	C
O	C	W	A	B
C	D	X	J	R
Y	X	E	M	Q
O	K	W	S	J
B	T	S	E	R

Color the
pencil.

E.D. Nixon and others got together to plan the strategy for a bus boycott. Many community organizations and churches helped spread the word. Flyers were also printed, telling of Rosa's arrest and urging people not to ride the buses on December 5.

The young Reverend Martin Luther King, Jr. also participated in the bus boycott.

This bus boycott became known as the famous Montgomery bus boycott. It lasted for 380 days!

The Supreme Court declared segregation of the Montgomery buses illegal and officially desegregated them on December 20, 1956.

BOYCOTT	ARREST	LAW

X	E	S	T	P
M	B	U	R	K
H	V	E	I	Y
U	S	I	G	K
I	G	T	H	A
A	K	S	T	O
B	P	L	S	M
R	A	T	H	K

Rosa lost her job as a seamstress as a result of the bus boycott. She and her husband continued to be harassed in Montgomery. In 1957, they decided to move to Detroit, Michigan to find work. In Detroit, they had a hard time finding jobs and were homeless for awhile.

Even through these rough times, Rosa remained active in the NAACP.

Put the following events in order.

_____ Rosa married Raymond Parks.

_____ Rosa was arrested and fined.

_____ Rosa moved to Detroit.

_____ Rosa refused to give up her bus seat.

In 1965, Rosa finally found steady work in the office of U.S. Congressman John Conyers, Jr., a civil rights leader in Congress.

Rosa continued to work for John Conyers, Jr. for over 20 years. Her husband, Raymond, died in 1977, two years before Rosa won the Springarn Medal for her work in civil rights. She continued to receive numerous awards and honors in recognition of her work.

In 1987, Rosa founded the Rosa and Raymond Parks Institute for Self-Development to provide career training for young people.

Color the picture of Rosa and her awards.

Rosa never had any children.

In 1992, Rosa published her autobiography *Rosa Parks: My Story*. In 1995, she took part in the Million Man March in Washington, D.C. where she gave an inspirational speech. Rosa died in her home on October 25, 2005.

In July of 1999, President Bill Clinton awarded Rosa the nation's highest civilian honor. To learn the name of this award, cross off every other letter below, starting with the letter B.

B C H O T N R G E R I E Z S P S Y I B
O V N M A K L O G X O E L Q D N M
R E A D I A G L U H P O B N E O W R

_ _ _ _ _ _ _ _ _ _ _ _

_ _ _ _   _ _ _ _ _

of   _ _ _ _ _ _

Glossary

autobiography: a story of one's own life, written by oneself

boycott: to join with others and refuse to buy, sell, or use something

civilian: a person who is not a member of the armed forces

harassed: to worry or trouble; to trouble by attacking again and again

segregation: forcing people of different racial groups to live apart from each other, go to separate schools, and use separate public facilities

Pop Quiz!

1. Rosa's mother was a:
   - ○ teacher
   - ○ nurse
   - ○ minister

2. Rosa volunteered for the:
   - ○ Sierra Club
   - ○ NAACP
   - ○ Humane Society

3. Rosa's arrest started the_____bus boycott.
   - ○ Philadelphia
   - ○ Atlanta
   - ○ Montgomery

4. Rosa and her husband moved from Alabama to:
   - ○ Indiana
   - ○ Florida
   - ○ Michigan

5. Rosa was awarded the Congressional Gold Medal of Honor in:
   - ○ 1950
   - ○ 1972
   - ○ 1999